Let's Learn About…

PIGS

By: Breanne Sartori

2

Introduction

Who doesn't know and love pigs! Their happy faces and pretty pink skin are very adorable. A lot of people think that pigs are dirty animals, but they're actually really clean! The pig we know and love (and eat!) has been domesticated over thousands of years. There are a lot of wild species of big that aren't so pretty – or friendly!

What Pigs Look Like

Pigs are big, round animals with four, short legs. They have a round face with a long, round nose called a snout. All pigs have tails that can be either curly or straight. They have big ears on top of their head that are almost square-shaped!

Feet

Each foot, called a trotter, has four toes that point downward. Each foot has a hoof which allows the big to walk across hard ground without hurting their feet. The middle two toes are webbed a little! This helps them keep their balance.

Teeth

Pigs have very strong, hardy teeth. Their teeth are coated in enamel, like human teeth, which protects them from diseases. All pigs have tusk teeth which are used to dig up food. But they need to make sure to wear them down so they don't grow too long!

Tusks

Many pigs also have tusks! These tusks stick out on either side of their snout, like horns. They are used to help dig up roots to eat. Tusks are also great weapons for self-defence!

Where Pigs Live

Pigs are found all over the world now that they have been domesticated. Wild pigs are native to Africa, Asia and parts of Europe. Depending on the species of wild pig, they can be found in either cool forests or hot deserts and grasslands.

Rolling in Mud

Pigs love to roll in mud! But it's not because they like to be dirty animals! They do it to keep themselves cool and protect themselves from the sun! Their fur is very fine, so their skin gets burnt very easily.

Cleanliness

Pigs are actually one of the cleanest animals around. They never go to the toilet near where they sleep or where they eat. Even newborn pigs will leave the nest to go to the toilet!

Walking

Did you know pigs walk on their tippy-toes? This is because their toes are designed pointing downward. Even though they have four toes, they only use the two middle ones to walk. The outer toes are just used to help them balance and hardly every touch the ground!

What Pigs Eat

Pigs are omnivores who will eat almost anything they find. In the wild they will eat fruit, berries, roots, tree bark and insects. Their favourite foods are roots, but they will scavenge whatever they can – they aren't fussy!

Social Life

Pigs are very social animals. In fact they form very strong bonds with each other. They love to be close to each other and touch each other a lot! When sleeping they also lie very close to each other.

Communication

Pigs are constantly talking to each other! Most of the time they will communicate with each other in the form of grunts and squeals. They are very peaceful and are never aggressive with each other. They are very quiet animals usually though.

Baby Pigs

You probably know that baby pigs are called piglets. But did you know that once a piglet is weaned, it's actually called a shoat? A baby pig will grow very quickly, doubling their weight in just a week!

Breeding

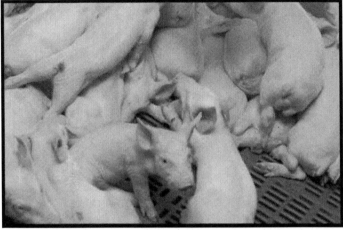

Pigs can have as many as seven piglets in each litter! The female will make a rough nest to give birth to her babies in. The piglets will spend their whole time in their nest with their mother next to them so that they can eat whenever they want.

The Life of a Pig

Piglets are often weaned by the time they are 3 months old, but they will stay with their parents until they are mature. A pig will be mature around 7 months old, which is when they can start to breed. Pigs can live for about 15 years, but surprisingly wild species can live longer – up to 20 years!

Predators

The most common predators of pigs in the wild are large cats like leopards and tigers! This is because there are so many of them! Wolves, hyenas, bears and even crocodiles are known to hunt wild pigs.

Other Dangers

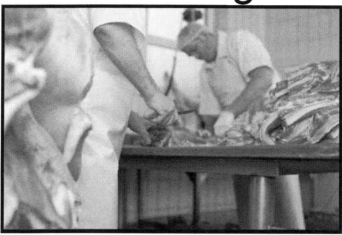

The biggest danger to pigs is, of course, humans. Domestic pigs are bred especially to be eaten! Wild pigs are also at risk from being hunted for their ivory tusks, not just their meat. The habitat of these animals is also being destroyed.

Defending Themselves

The tusks of pigs can be great weapons! They are long and can be very sharp and are used to stab or just push predators around. While pigs are usually very calm, they will fight if they or their babies are threatened. The male is much more capable of fighting than the female because their tusks are longer.

Domestic Pig

The domestic pig is the one we usually think of when talking about bigs. They are a light pink colour and covered in very fine hair. They don't have tusks because they have been purposely bred so that they don't have them. This is so farmers aren't accidentally hurt.

Warthog

The warthog has two sets of tusks! They have long ones on the bottom lip for foraging and fighting. They have smaller ones on the top lip which keep the bottom tusks sharp! These pigs are found in deserts and shrub-lands in Africa.

Wild Boar

The wild boar is native to Europe and Asia, but has been introduced into lots of other countries as well. Their fur is a lot longer than most pigs and is very shabby. Boars are nocturnal animals and not as social as the rest. Even though females live in herds, the males tend to live alone.

Made in the USA
San Bernardino, CA
23 April 2018